Cambridge English Readers

Level 3

Series editor: Philip Prowse

The Beast

Carolyn Walker

CAMBRIDGE

CAMBRIDGE UNIVERSITY PRESS
Cambridge, New York, Melbourne, Madrid, Cape Town, Singapore,
São Paulo, Delhi

Cambridge University Press
The Edinburgh Building, Cambridge CB2 8RU, UK

www.cambridge.org
Information on this title: www.cambridge.org/9780521750165

First published 2001
7th printing 2008

Printed in Italy by L.E.G.O. S.p.A.

A catalogue record for this publication is available from the British Library

ISBN 978-0-521-75016-5 paperback
ISBN 978-0-521-68657-0 paperback plus audio CD pack

Contents

Characters

Susie Blackmore: a photographer who lives in London.
Charlie Blackmore: Susie's husband.
Richard: has recently moved to Llandafydd village in Wales.
Tom Lloyd: a farmer who lives in Llandafydd.
Kathryn Lloyd: Tom's wife.

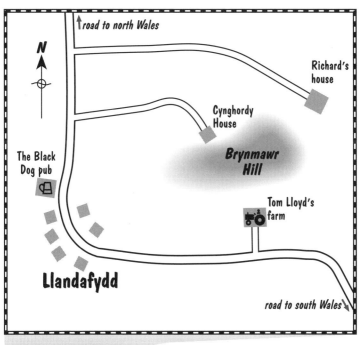

road to north Wales

N

Richard's house

Cynghordy House

Brynmawr Hill

The Black Dog pub

Tom Lloyd's farm

Llandafydd

road to south Wales

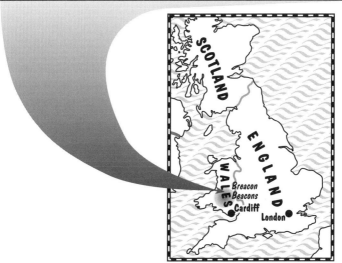

SCOTLAND

ENGLAND

WALES

Breacon Beacons

Cardiff

London

Chapter 1 *The zoo*

'Today,' Susie Blackmore thought to herself, 'is going to be another bad day.'

She was alone in her little flat in West London. It was the end of September 1999, the last quarter of the last year of the century. The millennium, in fact. The sun was coming through the window and outside the trees were moving slowly in the autumn wind. A bus came along the road, stopped outside the house and moved off again. Susie listened for a few moments to the traffic sounds outside her window. Life was going on as usual.

Slowly, Susie stood up and made herself some tea. She took it back to the table by the window and sat holding the cup. This was no good. She didn't want to do any work. The dream she'd had last night was still with her, following behind her like a ghost.

She'd started having bad dreams several weeks ago, the night after her father died. Sometimes in the dreams she was in a place she didn't know. She knew that she had to escape from something. She was very afraid of the dark, deathly thing that was chasing her. Often a voice called her name loudly in her dream and she woke up. Although it was a dream, she was sure that the voice was real.

She finished her tea and looked at her watch. It was just after ten o'clock. 'Come on,' she told herself. 'Time to go out, get moving.' She found her coat and camera and left a message on the telephone answering machine for her husband, Charlie: 'I've gone out to do a job. I'll be back around midday. Leave a message and I'll call you back.'

The underground station was fairly quiet at this time in the morning. She bought her ticket and waited for the train. Between stations, the train stopped for a few moments and Susie looked at the other travellers. She studied their faces in the glass in the window opposite. Outside the window, everything was black. She thought of her father again. She tried to see his face in the window glass as well. But his kind eyes and smile didn't come. Had she forgotten his face so soon? She felt a wave of sadness.

She'd felt so terrible when she got the phone call from the hospital. It had all happened very suddenly, they told her. Her father went to hospital very quickly by ambulance, but they couldn't help him. The doctor said he was very sorry. Now Susie felt like a small child again, lost in the big adult world. Well OK, she had Charlie, but that was different. Her mother had died when she was a baby. The only family she had left now were her cousins in Slovenia. But she didn't know her Slovene cousins very well. They phoned her when they heard about her father. It was the first time she had spoken to them since she was a child. His heart just stopped, she told them. No-one could do anything. It was very sudden.

She had dreams about her father, too. In last night's dream he was smiling. 'Don't worry about me,' he said. 'I'm fine.' He was back home in the village in Slovenia where he was born. He was having a great time, seeing old friends and family.

'I'll come and see you as soon as I get home,' he promised. Just as he used to when he was alive, every week.

In the dream she had thought, 'Ah, he isn't dead after all. It was all a terrible mistake.' And then she'd woken, and remembered.

She got out of the train at Regent's Park and walked towards the zoo. This was one of her favourite parts of the city. It was such a different place from the busy world of shops and business and London traffic. She liked to watch the animals as they played, ate or lay on the ground asleep.

The zoo wanted some photographs of the animals. You had to be very good in the photography business, and Susie knew she was good. But that was not enough. She had to work hard taking photographs. At the same time she had to find new jobs to do. She loved her work but it was a difficult life. She was beginning to feel tired of it. And now her father was gone. Was it time for a change? For the first time in her life, she wanted a child. A child for her father's lost life.

*   *   *

This morning there were not many visitors. She almost had the place to herself, except for the zoo keepers, who were giving food to the animals. Susie stopped to look at the grey wolves as they walked hungrily up and down. They were like large friendly dogs, really, not at all wild or dangerous. She remembered the stories her father used to tell her about the Volkodlak. It was a terrible thing, a sort of man-wolf-vampire who stole bad children away in the night and drank their blood. When she was little, of course, she thought the stories were true. She smiled as she thought about it.

She lifted up her camera. One of the wolves stopped

moving and watched her. Susie found herself looking back through the camera. The hair on her skin stood up and she felt suddenly afraid. She couldn't move. She felt sure that the animal wanted to tell her something.

The next thing she knew was that she was lying on the ground. The worried face of one of the zoo keepers was above her.

'Are you all right, love?' he asked. 'I've sent for the doctor.'

'Umm,' was all that she could say.

Chapter 2   *Voice of the Beast*

I sleep with my eyes open. My ears hear the smallest sound and I wake. If air moves softly over the hairs on my body, I will know that there is a living thing near me. Smells of animals brought by the wind can reach me over hundreds of kilometres.

Are you afraid of the dark? You are right to be afraid. We live in the darkness and there we do our work. You can be sure that we want only what is bad. Only what can hurt you. When you are feeling weak, we will know. Then we will watch you while you sleep, waiting for the time when we can take you into our darkness. In the night, we talk to you and call you to come to us. The knock on the door that wakes you in the night – that is one of us, come to invite you to a living death. Do not listen. Close your ears, if you want to escape with your life.

We have always been here. We have been here from the start of time.

Many thousands of years ago people ate with the gods. At that time, in Arcadia in Greece, there was a man called Lykaon. In Greek stories, Lykaon was the son of the first man on earth. He was the king of the people who lived on the hills and in the woods of Arcadia. But Lykaon was a man who did bad things, and one day the god Zeus heard about them. So he paid a surprise visit. Lykaon killed a child and gave it to Zeus to eat. Zeus was so angry that he turned Lykaon into a wolf.

Lykaon had to leave his people and live in the woods by himself.

He was half man and half wolf.

The sons of Lykaon, my brothers and I, have been on the earth all this time. But we left Arcadia and travelled the world. Each one of us went alone. We lived in hiding in many different places. Sometimes, we showed ourselves to people, but they were terribly afraid of us. They used guns and shot us with silver bullets. They made big fires and burnt us alive and cut off our heads.

But we did not die. We just changed. Into the undead.

We move around the earth in many forms. You do not see us but we are among you, in all parts of the world, from the east to the west, from the north to the south, in Venezuela, France, Mexico and Florida, from the Caucasus to the Alps, from Georgia to Greece, from the icy fields of Russia to the green hills of England. You can hear our cries if you listen hard. They are carried on the hot winds from the south and across the white mountains of the north.

There is nothing you can do to escape from us. You may think you can kill us with your silver bullets. But you cannot. We move from one body to another, from one place to another. We need blood and dead meat and we are always hungry. We will kill anything that lives: babies, cows, children, sheep, goats, chickens, men, women . . .

How can you know us? Well, what do you think you will see? Sometimes, for example, I am an animal of the night like a bat or a wolf or an owl. Or a wild black dog, like the dog that sits at the entrance to the Underworld. Sometimes I am the ghost that lies down next to you when you sleep. Or I am a beautiful young man or woman whom you want more than anything else in the world.

I am all of these things and I am none of them. I move between your world and mine as easily as a fish through water. You cannot understand how easily. You may see something moving in the corner of your eye. If you turn to look, there will be nothing there. Just a leaf blowing in the wind, you think. But I am following in the darkness behind you. I am your worst dream.

Chapter 3   *A holiday*

'Are you OK?' Charlie asked Susie that evening as they sat in their small kitchen. 'You're very quiet.' He watched her. Her dark, Eastern European eyes always made her face look white, but today she seemed whiter than usual. There were dark circles under her eyes.

'Yes, I'm fine. I'm not sleeping well at the moment, that's all,' Susie said. 'I keep having these dreams. It was about Dad last night. I thought he was alive again.' Her voice shook a little.

Charlie felt worried about Susie. Last August, after her father died, she'd seemed lost. She'd looked so ill that Charlie had made her go to the doctor. It was quite usual to feel bad after the death of a parent, the doctor had said. She would be better in a few weeks. He'd given her some pills to help her sleep. But today she seemed almost more afraid than sad, Charlie thought.

Susie didn't say any more. And Charlie didn't ask her to talk. He had always felt that there was a side of her that he could never understand. Although her mother was English and Susie had lived all her life in London, she still seemed a little foreign. Actually, this was what he'd liked about her in the first place, and now he loved her dearly. But sometimes he felt that he didn't know her.

Maybe they needed something else in their lives. A child? Charlie asked himself if a baby would help Susie feel better after the death of her father. He was nearly thirty now; a good age to be a father.'

'I think we should have a holiday,' he said to Susie suddenly. 'You know, relax a bit, get away from everything.'

'Well . . .' Susie started.

'We should spend some time together, you know,' Charlie said. 'We're both always so busy. Sometimes I don't see you for days.'

Susie looked at him. 'Yes, perhaps you're right,' she said slowly. 'We could find a house in the country somewhere. Somewhere completely different, a long way from London.'

'Good idea,' Charlie said. 'What about Wales? I used to go there for holidays when I was a child. There are some lovely little houses up in the hills.'

'Great! Let's do that,' said Susie. 'But there are one or two jobs I need to finish first.'

'Me too,' Charlie said. 'I can't get away until after next month. I've got a big show to organise.'

*   *   *

Two months later, on a cold grey Saturday in November, Charlie and Susie were driving along a narrow country road in the Welsh hills. They'd left London early in the morning and now it was nearly lunchtime. They seemed to be in the middle of nowhere.

'Are you sure this is the right way?' Charlie asked. The last houses had been in a village at least three kilometres before.

'Yes, I think so,' Susie replied, looking again at a hand-drawn map.

The road was full of holes and a thick line of grass was

growing down the middle. It led them through a dark wood and down a hill. Just as they started to go up again, a fox came out of the trees. It ran along the road in front of the car.

'Hey, look at that!' Susie cried. She'd never seen a wild fox before.

'Oh!' Charlie was just as surprised. The fox stopped for a moment and looked with cold interest at the people in the car. Then it continued along the road and suddenly turned to the right.

'It's showing us where to go!' Susie laughed. The fox disappeared into the woods just as, through the trees, they could see a dark stone building. 'Cynghordy House', a painted piece of wood said. At last, their holiday house.

Inside, the little house felt cold and the tall trees outside made it rather dark. The front door opened into a small kitchen. From there, a door led into the sitting-room where there was an old sofa and an armchair in front of a fireplace. Beyond the sitting-room was a light airy room which looked south. Looking out of the window, Susie could see that the ground rose towards a high round hill. At the foot of the hill there was a small wood, but the top was empty of trees. Two large birds were flying round and round in the empty sky above the hill.

'Charlie, come and look. What are those birds?' Susie called. Charlie looked over her shoulder.

'Red kites,' he said. 'They're very unusual in Britain. You only find them in a few places and this part of Wales is one of them. They're meat-eaters. There's probably some kind of dead animal down there, which is going to be their dinner.'

'Ugh! What a terrible thought!' said Susie.

'It says here that the nearest shops are in the village we came through. Llandafydd,' Charlie told her. He was looking at a piece of paper with information about the house. 'And there are a couple of pubs there too.'

'It's like an ice box in here,' Susie said. 'How do we heat the house?'

'Ah,' said Charlie. 'It says, "The wood-burning fire in the sitting-room heats the hot water and all the house." But it's OK,' he laughed as Susie's face fell. 'It says there's lots of wood already cut outside in the garage.'

'Let's light the fire, then,' Susie said. 'And I'm hungry. Why don't we go back to the village after that? We can have some lunch in a pub and do some shopping.'

'All right. Good idea.' Charlie went out to the car to bring in their suitcases.

Susie watched him. His thin blond hair was falling into his eyes. He was much taller than her. He had a way of moving his head down towards her when he spoke to her. Suddenly, she wanted to cry. These days the smallest things made her want to cry.

Red in the face and hot, Charlie put the last of their suitcases on the kitchen floor. 'That's it, thank God,' he said. 'What on earth have you got in that one? It's terribly heavy!'

'Just my camera and things, that's all,' she said. 'Can you help me with the fire? The wood won't burn.'

'Why can't women light fires? That's what I'd like to know.' Charlie smiled at her. He went into the sitting-room where he found an old newspaper. He began to put pieces of it into the fire.

Outside, the birds screamed in the sky and the wind shook the tall trees. Susie felt cold again. 'There must be a window open somewhere,' she thought, as the air moved softly against her short dark hair.

Chapter 4 *Voice of the Beast*

Let me tell you a story.

It was Midsummer's Eve in the year 1899. The moon was full over Brynmawr Hill in Central Wales. A farmer was out with his dog. He was waiting for the animal which had killed several of his sheep. A gun was under his arm. In the moonlight, he suddenly saw the sheep run across the field. Something large and dark was following them, moving fast. He held up his gun and shot. The thing cried out with a terrible sound, like a wolf, and stood up on its back legs. To the farmer, it seemed more than three metres tall. It was hurt, but it ran off on two legs down the hill into the woods.

The farmer's dog turned and ran for home as fast as it could. The farmer shot his gun into the trees a few times and then followed his dog back. His face was white. He was cold and afraid. When he arrived home, he said nothing to his wife about the thing in the woods. But that night he did not sleep.

The next morning the farmer's wife went into the village to do her shopping. Someone told her about something that had happened to the son of a rich family who lived near the village. Soon everyone was talking about the young man.

'What do you think?' the farmer's wife said to her husband when she returned. 'The boy has shot himself in the leg. He was playing with his gun and it went off by mistake. Really. He's nearly a man now. He's old enough to know better.' The farmer said nothing but only shook his head.

After a while, everyone forgot about what had happened to

the young man. Everyone except the farmer. He could not forget what he had seen on Brynmawr Hill. He noticed, too, that the young man had disappeared. No-one ever saw him again.

On the nights when he could not sleep, the farmer sat and wrote in a notebook. He wrote about that strange night on Midsummer's Eve.

After he died, a few years later, his wife found the notebook. When the story came out, everyone said the old farmer had been completely mad. Of course, people did not think that the story was true. But by that time the rich family had moved away and their large house was empty. Strangely, no-one wanted to buy it.

Why am I telling you all this?

Well, I was that young man.

After I was hurt, I travelled to that part of Europe which goes from Hungary in the east, across Austria, Slovenia and the north of Italy. There I lived with others of my kind, in the hills and mountains, until I was better. Then I went south to Greece. I visited Mount Lykaon, the place where Lykaon was changed into a wolf, the place where it all began.

I was careful, hiding in woods all the time. I took people's sheep or goats to eat only when there were not enough wild animals. For many years, I was not seen again but then I started to get careless. I went to many places in Europe. A soldier saw me in Germany in 1988 – outside a place called Morbach. I know that people tell stories about this.

Ah, but now I have returned. I have come back to the hills and old woodlands of Wales. This is my home, the right place, I think, to welcome in the new millennium.

Chapter 5   *In the Black Dog pub*

'Let's try that one, shall we?' Charlie said. He was looking at a pub on the road going into the village of Llandafydd. They stopped next to a dirty old van which was outside the pub. In the back of the van was a sheep, which looked unhappily at them through the van window. They walked up to the front entrance of the pub. Charlie tried to open the heavy door, pulling first then pushing it. It opened suddenly and he almost fell inside.

The pub wasn't busy, although it was lunchtime. Susie went quickly to a seat by a welcoming fire. Charlie walked up to the woman behind the bar and asked for two beers and a menu. The room was very quiet.

A man at the bar watched as Charlie sat down opposite Susie. After a while, he turned back to the landlady behind the bar and started talking to her, speaking in Welsh. Susie and Charlie studied the menu while the strange sounds of the foreign language made it hard to think.

Looking up for a moment, Susie's eyes were caught by a picture on the other side of the room. In front of dark moonlit hills, a black dog with strange red eyes was looking at her. As she studied the picture, a man who was sitting below it stood up. He walked slowly towards the bar with his empty glass.

He looked across at Susie. He had dark greying hair and very white skin, like a plant that has grown without light. She found herself looking into his clear blue eyes. She had an uncomfortable feeling that she knew him from somewhere. Suddenly, she did not want to be there, in that pub, in Wales.

'Same again, Richard?' the landlady said to the man.

'Yes, please,' Richard replied. 'Problems, Tom?' he asked the man at the bar, a farmer.

'I'm afraid so, yes,' Tom answered, in English now. 'Found two of my sheep dead today. Looked terrible, they did. Tongues gone, ears and noses bitten off. Never seen anything like it.' His voice became quieter. 'And no blood. There was no blood. Not on the ground. Not on the body.'

'It was probably just a fox or a dog, wasn't it, Tom?' the landlady said.

Tom the farmer shook his head. 'Oh no,' he said. 'There's no animal on earth that kills like that.'

'It's the Beast of Brynmawr,' Richard told the landlady. 'It's come back again.'

'Oh, come on now!' the landlady said. 'There's no such thing.'

'Of course there is,' Richard said, smiling. 'It's a werewolf, everyone knows that. Half man, half wolf. Last seen on Brynmawr Hill a hundred years ago.' The landlady laughed loudly.

Susie and Charlie couldn't help listening to this conversation. 'I think I'll just have a cheese sandwich,' Susie said quietly to Charlie.

'Well, I'm going to have steak and chips. I'm really hungry,' Charlie told her, and went up to the bar.

'On holiday are you, then?' the landlady asked as she took Charlie's order. She seemed friendly, Charlie thought.

'Yes,' he answered. 'We're staying up at Cynghordy House for a couple of weeks.'

'Aha. On Brynmawr Hill.' She smiled and looked at Richard and Tom. 'They'd better watch out for the Beast of Brynmawr, then, hadn't they?'

Richard laughed. Tom didn't. 'It's no joke,' he said in a low voice.

*   *   *

After lunch, Susie and Charlie went into the centre of Llandafydd. It was a quiet little village with only a few shops: a small supermarket, a post office, a tea shop and a shop which sold presents for holidaymakers to take home. Susie wanted to look in the tourist shop. She bought a plate with a red kite on it.

It was getting dark by the time they arrived back at Cynghordy House. But the wood fire was still burning and the house was warmer.

'OK, what are we going to do now, then?' Charlie said. He was not used to being on holiday. Usually he spent most of his waking hours at work, always on the phone, talking and talking, or on the computer. He never stopped moving.

Susie began to put their shopping away in the cupboards in the kitchen. 'I'm tired,' she said after a while. 'I think I'll lie down for a bit. Let's have something to eat soon and have an early night, shall we?'

Charlie went outside to get in some more wood. The cold November light was beginning to go. Above the hill the red kites were still flying round and round. To the east a full moon was rising slowly up into the night sky. Charlie was surprised to see that this moon was an orange-red colour, not the usual yellow-white. He remembered the words, a 'hunter's moon' from when he was a child. Was this a 'hunter's moon'?

Chapter 6 *Voice of the Beast*

Now I look from my window and see that the light is going from the earth. Tonight the moon will be up for most of the night. Its silver light will fall like soft rain on the woods and trees, on the tops of the hills. Soon I will feel the cold night wind on my face, the air moving through the hairs on my head and arms and back. I will listen to the sound of my feet as they walk on the wet earth and the grass. I will hear the small sounds of animals as they move quickly to get out of my way.

I am going out tonight.

You ask why? I will tell you.

Some visitors have arrived. I watched them come through the woods. I saw them looking around in the strange new place. They are city people. Here, they are unsure. They move carefully.

Then later they were in the pub. Death has touched her with its cold fingers. I could see that in her eyes. Now she is afraid of the darkness that is following her.

But also there is something in her face that I know. I have seen that face before, I'm sure. Maybe in Greece? Northern Italy? Maybe in a mountain village somewhere? She interests me. I cannot stop thinking about her. I want her to come with me, to be with me.

I know she is ready to come into my world. But she does not know it herself yet. When I tell her, she will understand what she must do. But I must be careful. The time must be right . . .

First, I will go and welcome her, take a present. I must make myself ready.

I walk across the room in the darkness to the fireplace. Daylight makes me weak and ill. The soft silvery light of the moon is what I like. From the wall, I take my belt. It is large and heavy, black and silver. On the silver there is the face of a dog. The dog that sits at the entrance to the Underworld.

I put the belt carefully on the floor in front of the fire. I get down on my knees and put both my hands on the belt. Softly, I repeat the words that I must say. The words are in a language no man or woman can speak. I feel the heat from the fire on my face. In the centre of the fire I watch my thoughts come and go.

After a while, after all the words are finished, I stand up and put on the belt. Immediately, my arms and legs start to feel strong. I look towards the blackening sky and give a wild shout. Then, in one great jump, I am gone from the room through the open window.

The night is cold but I do not feel it. I will not feel it until I become a man again. I touch the belt around the middle of my body. I will know what to do when the moment comes.

Chapter 7   *The present*

It was still dark when Susie woke up. Looking at her clock she saw it was three o'clock in the morning. She lay in bed in the darkness for a while, Charlie's warm body next to her. It was strange that she'd woken so suddenly. Had someone knocked at the door and called her name? Or was it just a dream, as usual?

Suddenly, her body gave a jump. There was a small noise at the bedroom window. Was something trying to get in? The noise came again, and again.

'Charlie, there's something outside,' she said. Her voice seemed very loud to her.

'Um, what? Go back to sleep, there's nothing there,' Charlie said sleepily.

Susie sat up. Outside the wind had become stronger and was blowing noisily through the trees. She climbed out of bed and went to the window. Pulling back the curtain she could see that a tree was moving against the glass. So it was the tree that was making the noise. Outside, in the light of the full moon, the trees and grass were waving and shaking in the wind. Anything could be hiding in the darkness.

Susie put on the lights and walked round the house, looking into every room. There was nothing there, of course. It was just the house itself, maybe, moving in the wind like a boat at sea, which had made the knocking noise. She got back into bed, moved close to Charlie and went back to sleep.

When Susie woke the next morning she could see the sunlight through the thin curtains in the bedroom. Charlie was asleep still. 'It must be late,' she thought. She decided to get up, make some breakfast for both of them and bring it back to bed.

Downstairs the fire was nearly out. They'd used all the wood the night before so she decided to get some more from the garage. She pulled on a coat over her nightclothes and put on some shoes. She went to open the door. Strangely, the door didn't move at first. Something seemed to be holding it. She gave it a pull.

As the door opened, Susie heard herself scream. It was a strange sound, which came from somewhere far inside her. She had never made a noise like that before in her life.

'Charlie, Charlie!' She couldn't move.

There was the sound of feet on wood as Charlie came running down the stairs.

'What on earth is the matter?' Charlie said.

'Oh my God . . .' He saw the open door and the large and terrible thing on the ground, half in and half out of the kitchen. 'Whatever is *that* doing there?'

'What is it, Charlie?' Susie found it difficult to speak.

'It's a dead sheep,' Charlie replied, after a few moments. 'Listen, you go back to bed and I'll do something with it,' he added.

The sheep's body was not pretty to look at. The mouth was open. Charlie couldn't help seeing that the tongue wasn't there. The sheep was cut open from the throat down under the body as far as the back legs. But the cut was clean and there was no blood.

Looking more brave than he felt, Charlie took hold of

the two back legs. He pulled the body out of the kitchen, and then across the road outside the house and into the field opposite.

'We ought to tell somebody about it,' he thought. 'The farmer, probably.'

He asked himself why the sheep was there. Did it just die there? Or did an animal leave it by the door? He tried not to think about who, or what, had put the sheep there. Perhaps there really was a Beast of Brynmawr. Anyway, he felt sick.

He went back into the house, made a cup of tea and took it up to his wife. Susie was lying in the bed. Her pretty face, with her dark hair cut like a boy's, looked small and white.

'God, Charlie, that was one of the worst things I've ever seen,' she said. 'I heard some strange noises in the night, you know. I thought I heard someone knocking at the door. Do you think someone is trying to play some sort of terrible joke on us?'

'Susie, you mustn't think about it. It was probably just a fox or something. Maybe it decided it would eat its dinner outside our back door. Come on, let's try and forget it. We're here to have a holiday and enjoy ourselves.'

'Well, yes. OK. You're right. I'll try,' Susie said. But she could still see the cold eye of the sheep looking up at her from the kitchen floor.

'Do you think the Beast of . . . ?' she began again.

'No,' Charlie spoke quickly. 'I don't. Forget about it. There's no such thing.'

Chapter 8   *A walk on Brynmawr Hill*

After breakfast, Charlie said, 'Look, it's a wonderful day. Let's go for a walk.'

'OK, then. I'll bring my camera.' Susie tried to sound happy.

They walked towards the big round hill, which was opposite the house. The day was fine, with a soft autumn sun which came and went behind thick grey clouds. It wasn't cold but there was a wind. They were pleased that they had their jackets.

'Charlie,' Susie said, as they climbed the grassy hillside. 'Do you think this is Brynmawr Hill? You know, the place they talked about in the pub? Where someone saw a werewolf a hundred years ago?'

Charlie smiled. 'Probably. Come on, let's just get to the top,' he said.

From the top of the hill, the country looked beautiful. All around they could see the great dark hills of central Wales. The clouds moved slowly across the sky and, on the lower parts of the hills, the sun on the grass looked like watery gold. The light was perfect and Susie put up her camera as fast as she could. She couldn't wait to take some photographs.

'Listen,' Charlie said. 'I'm going to walk on a little way while you're doing that.'

'OK. I'll take a few photos from here, then I'll go over towards that place there.' Susie was looking at a small hill several hundred metres from where they were standing. 'I'll wait for you there,' she said.

Charlie walked quickly, planning to go in a large circle. He looked back, but Susie had disappeared.

The dead sheep had worried both of them quite a lot. They had not talked about it again. But Charlie could still see the body, lying there, with bits of it missing and one eye open. Also, he realised, because there had been no blood coming from the animal, it had probably died somewhere else. But who, or what, had put it outside their house? He couldn't stop thinking about it. He knew that Susie was finding it hard to forget as well. It wasn't a good start to their holiday.

Charlie stood for a moment on the hill. Far below him, he saw that some sheep were running across one of the fields. He watched as the white animals moved in a group across the large green field. The sounds of the sheep rose up towards him, carried on the wind. Then he saw why they were running: something was chasing them. It stopped to sit and watch the animals. Then it ran on and stopped again. A dog, Charlie thought. Was it possible that a dog had left the sheep at their door? He didn't know much about dogs.

Just then, the clouds above him turned a dark grey, the wind got stronger and rain came down in great fat drops. He'd better go and find Susie.

When Charlie arrived at the small hill, Susie was lying down. Charlie was surprised to see that she was asleep. Her camera was on the ground. It looked as if she'd dropped it.

'Susie, Susie!' Charlie shook her. 'What on earth are you doing? It's raining. Your camera's getting wet. Wake up.'

Susie opened her eyes and looked at Charlie. For a moment, Charlie saw something in her eyes that he had never seen before. She was terribly, terribly afraid.

'Are you OK?' he said. 'Why did you go to sleep? Are you OK?'

It was a few moments before Susie seemed to wake up. Charlie was really worried now. She looked so strange.

'No, I'm not OK. Well, maybe I am. I don't know. I was just standing here, taking a picture of that big tree across there. See? When I looked through the camera, I had the strangest feeling. I tried to move but I just couldn't. I felt as if I was in fast moving water. I couldn't make my legs move forward. Then there was a cold, icy wind and I heard an animal sound, kind of like a wolf and . . . then everything went black. Charlie, I hope there's nothing wrong with me? Am I going mad?'

Charlie looked at her unhappily. The horror of the dead sheep had clearly made her ill.

'Let's get back to the house. We're both wet through and it's terribly cold in this wind. Come on, let's go,' he replied softly.

Chapter 9 *An accident*

A few days later, Susie looked at the sitting-room window where the rain water was still running down the glass. They'd been nowhere since that first day. She hadn't wanted to do anything much. She just felt like sitting and reading. Or looking at the fire, putting on the wood, and thinking.

'Charlie, let's go out tonight,' Susie said suddenly. 'Let's go to the pub, shall we?'

'OK, if you want. The Black Dog?' he said. 'We'd better go soon. There's going to be snow later.'

'How do you know that?' Susie asked.

'Heard it on the car radio just now. I was mending that light. You know, that light on the front of the car.'

It was already dark by the time they started out for the pub. Susie watched her husband as he drove down the little road through the woods. In the yellow of the car lights, she could see he looked serious. He was thinking about something. What was it? Then she thought about who would be in the pub tonight. The farmer, perhaps? Or the man called Richard?

'Oh no. Look. It's starting to snow already!' Charlie said.

'Oh, so it is.' Susie could see little bits of snow caught in the lights of the car. The snow came flying towards them as they drove along. 'It's not very heavy,' she said.

They turned onto the main road into Llandafydd. Now they were driving into the wind and here the snow was falling fast.

'Perhaps we should go back,' Charlie said. 'It's getting quite thick.'

'It's only a little way now,' Susie said. 'We're nearly there. We could just have a quick drink and then go home.'

'Well, all right, but it's getting difficult to see.' Charlie sounded worried. The snow was coming towards the car in thick straight lines. He moved forward to look through the hole in the snow on the car window.

Just then, Susie saw something. 'Watch out!' she screamed. Something large and dark was moving towards them in the falling snow. It looked like a person, walking along the white line in the middle of the road.

Then the car lights went out.

'What the . . . ?' Charlie said. He tried to stop the car but on the snow it just went faster. There was a crashing, screaming sound of metal as they hit something.

A little while later, Susie opened her eyes. At first everything was black. Her head hurt a little. Then she saw that their car was no longer on the road. They'd hit a tree. The tree seemed to be half inside the car, on Charlie's side. In the darkness, she couldn't see what was Charlie and what was tree. The only sound was the wind in the trees. There was no-one else around.

'Charlie?' Susie touched his arm. There was no answer. 'Charlie?' Was he dead? What should she do? Should she try to get him out of the car? Was the car going to catch fire? Just then a soft noise, almost like a voice, came from the other side of the road and she looked across. A dark thing moved between the trees. She couldn't see if it was a person or an animal. It disappeared quickly.

A small sound came from Charlie. Thank God, he wasn't

dead after all. At the same time, car lights appeared along the road. She must get out and get help.

Outside on the road, her legs shook and she couldn't stand. She sat down suddenly in the snow. A Land Rover stopped and a voice said, 'Are you all right?'

'No,' Susie said. 'We need a doctor. My husband's hurt. Badly, I think.' She found that she was crying.

The man got out and helped Susie to stand up.

'Now then, I'm sure he's all right, my dear.' Susie saw that the farmer from the pub was looking worriedly at her. She remembered that his name was Tom.

'I've got a mobile phone in my car . . .' Susie began.

'That's OK. You come and sit in my Land Rover where it's warm, now,' Tom said. 'I'll go and have a look at your husband. And I'll get your phone.'

Tom took a blanket from the back of his car and went across the road. 'What terrible luck,' Susie thought. 'Why does Charlie always try to mend things himself?' She was always telling him to take the car to a garage and not to do it himself. 'He probably did something stupid,' she thought, 'to the lights in the car, so they went out.'

Had there been a person on the road? It wasn't possible, she thought. Perhaps it had been an animal. Or nothing at all. Just the way the light fell.

From her seat inside the Land Rover, Susie could hear low voices. Charlie must be awake, then. Tom returned after a while and said to Susie, 'It's OK, my dear. Your husband says his arm and leg hurt. But he's not too bad. He's probably just broken something. I'm afraid I don't know how to use these things.' He gave Susie her phone.

'You call 999 and then we can get your husband to a hospital.'

Her hands shaking, Susie pushed the numbers. 'Could you talk, please?' she asked Tom. 'I can't explain where we are.'

Tom spoke into the phone and then turned to Susie. 'Not long to wait,' he said. 'They'll be here soon. No, my dear, you stay here now,' he said as Susie started to get out of the Land Rover. 'I'll go and see if your husband's OK.'

Tom went back to the crashed car. It seemed a long time before he returned.

Susie was cold and afraid. How badly hurt was Charlie? She started to think about the worst things possible. Perhaps he would die? 'This is terrible,' she thought. 'I must go and see him.' She got out and stood by the Land Rover in the falling snow. Starting to walk across the road, she suddenly felt sick and her legs shook. She wasn't hurt but she felt so weak after the crash. She couldn't walk any further. She went slowly back to the Land Rover.

Then after a time the farmer came back and started to talk to her.

'On holiday, then, are you?' Tom asked.

'Yes,' Susie began. It was difficult to talk but she tried to be friendly. 'We're staying up in Cynghordy House. We were on our way to the Black Dog for a drink.'

'Oh yes,' Tom said. 'I remember now. You came into the pub a few days ago, didn't you?'

'Yes,' Susie said. 'We'd just arrived. I'm Susie Blackmore.'

The farmer smiled. 'Tom Lloyd. Pleased to meet you,' he replied.

Just then another car arrived and a man's voice asked if he could help. No, Tom told him, everything was all right. They had phoned and help was on the way. The car drove off again.

'Going to the pub, he is, I expect,' Tom said. 'He's new around here, Richard is. But he seems nice enough. You know, quite friendly. He's bought an old house which he's working on, so he says.'

Feeling a little better now, Susie asked, 'Was he in the pub the other day? You know, when Charlie and I were there?'

'Ah, yes. I believe he was,' Tom said.

They didn't speak for a bit. Then Susie saw, with some surprise, that there was a gun on the seat next to her.

'Do you shoot for sport, then?' she asked Tom.

'No,' he replied. 'I only shoot animals when I need to. Foxes, birds, and so on. And dogs, too, if they go after my sheep.'

'We found a dead sheep outside our front door a few days ago,' Susie said, remembering suddenly. 'It was very strange. We think something put it there. And ate bits of it too. Perhaps it was one of yours?'

'Maybe. I've lost five sheep now. There's something out there, I'm sure. Something that's very hungry and very large,' Tom said in a low voice. 'But I'm going to find it and kill it.' Susie could hear that he was very angry.

He looked at Susie for a moment and then took something from his pocket. He gave it to Susie. It was small and made of metal and lay heavily on her hand. It was a bullet.

'It's silver,' Tom said softly.

Chapter 10 *Voice of the Beast*

So far so good. That was well done. My plan is working well. I'm good at this. I'm patient and I think of everything. I know how to take one small step at a time. I know how to get what I want. Time means nothing to me. I can wait and wait for the right moment. It is like taking a photograph of a child or an animal. You must think hard, think of nothing else. You must know what will happen before it does. Or it is like flying a plane, or sailing a boat in a strong wind. A little touch here, a touch there, and everything will keep going in a straight line to the end.

The husband is not there now. He is hurt but I don't care. He is hurt just enough. Enough to keep him in the hospital, away from her. But not so badly that she will be worried about him. I don't want her to think too much about him. I want her to be happy to talk to me.

Things will be difficult for her now. She needs someone who can help her to do everything, the small everyday things. She is weak because the darkness is getting nearer and she knows it. Before, the darkness was only in her dreams. Now she feels it close behind her when she is awake and she is afraid. She is alone and she needs someone she can talk to. I am going to help her. She will talk to me because I will listen to her. Not like her husband. He does not know how to listen. Little by little. Step by step. That's the way to do it.

Chapter 11 *An unexpected visitor*

It was past ten o'clock at night when Tom finally left Susie in the little kitchen of Cynghordy House. She couldn't stay in the hospital with Charlie so Tom had driven her back. 'How kind and helpful Tom is,' she thought. She sat down at the table and looked at the white walls, the cupboards, the table, the fridge. Nothing moved. She felt strange in the thick quietness without Charlie. In London she didn't mind being alone, but here, in this house, she was uncomfortable. She knew she was afraid.

Now Charlie was in hospital with a broken leg and a broken arm. He was lucky not to have a broken neck. Poor Charlie. They said he had to stay in hospital for at least a week.

'Poor me, too,' she thought. 'What am I going to do now? I haven't got a car. Whose idea was it to have a holiday, anyway? What a wonderful holiday this is. Here I am in this house by myself on a cold, wet Welsh mountain in the middle of nowhere. I can't even walk to Llandafydd from here. There's no-one near, and what if . . . ' She stopped quickly before she could finish that thought.

'Well, anyway, I've got my mobile phone and at least there's Tom,' she told herself. 'He's been very kind.'

Tom had told her that he lived on the other side of the hill. She could ring him any time if she needed anything. He would try to come the next morning to see her. But he had a lot to do and he wasn't sure if he'd have time.

Anyway, she could call a taxi from Llandafydd to take her to the hospital.

She felt safer, thinking of Tom. She remembered the gun that she'd seen in his Land Rover. When he'd shown her the silver bullet, she hadn't understood at first. Then she had remembered the stories her father used to tell her. Tom didn't really think that a werewolf was killing his sheep. Did he?

She had asked him if he was joking. But he had just smiled and said, 'You never know, do you? You can't be sure . . .' She couldn't believe he was serious.

'Where my father came from,' she'd told him lightly, 'they believe that when a werewolf dies, it turns into a vampire. You can't kill them, you know. It's impossible. They just change into something else.'

'Do they really?' Tom had said.

'Of course, it's stupid,' she told herself now. 'Vampires and werewolves are just stories.' She got up to look at the fire in the sitting-room. She thought of the time on Brynmawr Hill, and the time at the zoo. But the danger wasn't real. There was nothing out there. It was only in her head. And she must fight it. She wished Charlie was there.

'Oh, no!' she said, aloud. The fire had gone out. That meant no hot water, and the house was cold now, too. And, of course, there was no wood in the box either.

'OK,' she thought, 'let's see if I can do this by myself . . .'

She picked up the wood box and opened the front door. She left the door open so that she could see a little and went out to the garage.

When the wood box was full, she stood up again to go back inside. Just then, she suddenly realised that someone or something was near her and was moving towards her in the dark.

She screamed and dropped the box. Pieces of wood fell everywhere. She stood still and couldn't move.

'Oh, I'm terribly sorry,' a friendly voice said. She knew the voice at once. It was Richard. The man from the pub.

'I made you jump, didn't I?' he went on. 'I just came to see if you were OK. I thought you might need something. Tom told me it was you two who were in the accident. I saw it on my way to the pub earlier tonight.' He made it sound like a question.

'Yes,' Susie said. 'I know. I saw it was you. It's kind of you to come. I'm fine. But Charlie's in hospital with a broken arm and a broken leg. Some holiday!'

'I'm so sorry. Poor Charlie,' Richard said. 'Here, let me help you pick up the wood.'

'Thanks,' Susie said. She added, 'I didn't hear you drive up or anything.'

'No, I walked the last bit,' Richard answered. 'The snow's quite bad on this road and I didn't want to have any trouble with the car. I haven't got a Land Rover like the farmers round here . . .'

'Well . . . would you like to come in?' Susie said, unsure what to do. He could help her with the fire anyway. And it would be nice to talk to someone for a bit.

She made them both a cup of tea while Richard lit the fire. The room soon started to feel warmer. Susie found herself talking to Richard as if he was an old friend. She told him about her life in London, her father, her family in Slovenia, her work. While she talked, he smiled at her and listened. She'd never talked like this before to a man she didn't know. He made her feel that everything she said was important and interesting.

She realised that he was very good-looking, in an unusual way. His blue eyes watched her while she spoke. It was strange how comfortable she felt. He was so easy to talk to. She might almost fall in love with him.

Suddenly, Susie realised what she was doing. Charlie was in hospital and here she was with a strange man in the house. How could she possibly be thinking of such a thing?

'Er . . . I'm afraid I'll have to go to bed now,' Susie said.

'Of course, I'm terribly sorry. How stupid of me, it's late,' Richard said. 'You must be very tired. I'd better go. Look, if you like, I could take you in to the hospital to see Charlie tomorrow. I've got to go into town anyway.'

'Oh well, that's very kind. Yes, please,' Susie said.

'I'll come and pick you up about twelve, then?' Richard said.

'That would be wonderful. Thanks very much. See you tomorrow,' she replied.

When Susie got into bed, she realised that she was very tired. But in the night, the dreams started again. A voice called to her. 'Come with me,' it said. In the dream, she knew the voice but she couldn't quite say whose it was.

Suddenly, she was awake. Outside, there was a kind of scream. 'It must be an animal caught by something,' Susie thought. It came again, and then again, a hopeless, deathly scream. She pulled the blankets over her head to shut out the noise.

Chapter 12   *Richard's house*

Looking out of her window the next morning, Susie saw that dark bits of grass were showing above the snow on the fields. On the road, the snow was quite thin. It wasn't as bad as she'd thought last night. She remembered that Richard was coming later to take her to the hospital. He would be able to drive right up to her house this time.

She phoned the hospital. The nurse said Charlie was fine, but he'd had an uncomfortable night. Susie told the nurse she would go to visit him later. She wasn't sure when.

Her phone rang. 'Hello, my dear,' a woman's voice said. 'It's Kathryn Lloyd. I'm Tom's wife. Tom asked me to call you. I'm afraid Tom's had to go out. He won't be able to come up to your house this morning. Are you all right now? Do you need anything?'

'No, it's OK,' Susie said. 'I'm fine. I'm going in to the hospital later. Richard is going to take me.'

'Richard?' Kathryn asked.

'Yes,' Susie said, realising that she didn't know Richard's family name. 'Er . . . Tom knows him. He's new in the village, Tom said. Anyway, Richard saw the accident and he came here last night to see if we were all right.'

'Ah, that was kind of him,' Kathryn said. 'Well, that's OK, then.'

*   *   *

Richard arrived at about midday, as he had said he would.

'Hello, there,' he said, smiling. 'How are you?'

'Fine,' Susie replied. She was pleased to see him.

'Let's go then, shall we?' he said. 'I'm afraid I forgot to bring my wallet with me. So we'll have to go back to my house. Do you mind? It's not far. In fact the house is only about a kilometre from here, over the hill. By road, you have to go back down to the main road and take the next turning. But it doesn't take very long.'

'No problem,' Susie said.

'Anyway, I'll show you my house. I'm sure you'll find it interesting.'

'Oh?' Susie wanted to know more.

'Yes.' Richard talked on, smiling warmly at Susie. 'Actually, it used to be my family's house a long time ago. When I came here for a visit one day, I found that the person who owned it wanted to sell it. I decided to buy it immediately.'

'Oh, so where did you live before, then?' Susie asked.

'Well, Europe, for a number of years. I was there on business. But I got tired of always moving and living out of a suitcase. I decided to stop working for a bit. I'd made enough money not to have to. And I've got enough to spend some on the house, too.'

'How nice,' Susie said, thinking how nice it would be not to have to work. But she wouldn't want to live on top of a Welsh mountain for the rest of her life. Too quiet. No-one around to speak to.

'Oh look,' she said as they passed a group of men in dark jackets standing by the side of the road. They wore hats and boots and were carrying guns. They were looking across a field towards some woods. 'Do you think they're hunting for the Beast of Brynmawr?' She smiled at Richard.

'Probably,' he said. 'But I don't think they'll find it at this time of day, do you?'

'No,' she agreed, laughing. 'It's probably asleep somewhere.'

They drove round a corner and Richard said, 'There it is.'

'Oh, goodness!' Susie cried. 'For a moment I thought you meant the Beast! Is that really your house?'

Ahead of them at the end of the road she saw a beautiful stone building. There were ten windows on the top floor and eight on the ground floor. In the centre was a large front door with a pretty roof over it. It was a very big house, built in the eighteenth century probably, Susie thought. It must be the house of a rich family. She hadn't expected this.

'Yes, it needs a lot of work,' Richard said.

'Does it?' Susie replied.

And as they got closer she could see that many of the windows had no glass. The front wall of the house seemed to be all that was there. If the wind blew, it might just fall down, like a building made of cards.

'So . . . you're actually living here?' she asked.

'Well, yes, there are a couple of rooms that are OK,' Richard said. 'It's not very comfortable, but I don't mind.'

He stopped by the front door and they got out.

'Come on,' he said. 'I'll show you round.'

Going through the great front door, Susie found herself in a large room with a stone floor. Some stairs led up to the first floor, but large holes showed where several steps were missing.

Richard smiled. 'I don't think we'll try that way, follow me.' He led her through several large rooms. Everywhere there were stones and dirt.

'Nearly there,' Richard said. They seemed to be walking for ages. Susie felt a drop of water on her head. She looked up. There was no floor above her. She could see the sky through the holes in the roof.

They went up some narrow stairs, past glassless windows, which looked down over the road. Finally, Richard opened a door into a room which felt quite warm. A fire was burning and there were chairs and a sofa.

'Have a seat,' Richard said. 'Would you like some coffee?'

'Er . . .' Really, Susie wanted to get to the hospital to see Charlie. What should she say?

'I've just remembered something else that I haven't done,' Richard said, before she could answer. 'I'm sorry. It's going to take me a moment or two. Why don't you sit down? I'll bring you some coffee while you wait. Then we'll get going again. OK?' He looked at her.

'Well, OK then. Yes, some coffee would be great,' Susie said, sitting on one of the rather dirty chairs near the fire.

Richard went out and Susie looked around her. On the dark wood walls, there were large pictures of men and women from years ago. There was a man who looked a little like Richard, she realised. Were these people his family? She felt uncomfortable with all these dead people looking at her. They made her think of the pictures in horror films where the eyes move. She laughed at herself.

Perhaps she should phone the hospital again? She could tell them that she would be in to see Charlie very soon. She opened her handbag.

'Oh, I'm so stupid,' she said to herself. The phone was not there. Of course! She'd left it on the kitchen table in Cynghordy House.

Richard came back with her coffee. Giving her the cup, he went to stand with his back to the fire.

'Thanks,' Susie said. 'Um, do you have a phone I could use? To phone the hospital?'

'No,' he almost shouted. 'There's no phone here.' Then he became quiet; his face had lost the friendly smile. He seemed to be waiting for something. Suddenly, everything had changed. The room was deathly quiet. Susie looked at the fire and drank her coffee.

A strange light came into Richard's blue eyes as he watched Susie drink. She started to feel very sleepy and she sat back on the chair. Her eyes were closing. She tried hard to keep them open. Richard stood still in front of the fire. She saw that he was wearing a large black belt with silver on it.

She looked up at Richard's face. 'He's got a beard,' she thought to herself. 'That's strange. He didn't have one before . . .'

Then the dream started.

*   *   *

She is looking at the dark, deathly Thing that has been following her in her dreams all this time. The face is

46

hidden. A hand takes hers. She knows very well whose it is. She feels terribly afraid.

'You are one of us. You know that, don't you?' She knows the voice as well as her own.

'No, I'm not. I will not listen to you. I will not,' she cries.

'I knew when you came here. You came to find me, didn't you?' the voice continues. It will not stop.

'No, no, I didn't. I don't know you,' she says. 'Take me to Charlie, please. Please!'

'You don't really want Charlie,' the voice tells her. 'You are mine. You know that in your heart.'

And she feels herself beginning to move towards him. He is right, perhaps. She will do anything he wants. She cannot stop herself . . .

Chapter 13   Escape

When Susie woke up, the room was in darkness. A small light was coming from the fireplace where the fire was still burning a little. A large white moon could be seen through the window.

What time was it?

Susie stood up to look at her watch in the moonlight. As she got to her feet, her head started to hurt badly, right between the eyes. Quickly, she sat down again. Was she ill? Why did she feel so bad?

And where was she?

She had had a terrible dream. The worst ever. But it wasn't real. It was just a dream.

Or was it?

Looking around she saw that she was in a place she did not know. Not the flat in London. Not the holiday house. Where then? There were some large pictures on the walls.

Ah, Richard, of course. In his house, that was where she must be. Had she fallen asleep here? They were going to see Charlie, weren't they? What had happened? Where was Richard?

Trying hard, she remembered having a cup of coffee and feeling sleepy. Then she thought of something and began to be afraid. Perhaps Richard had drugged her. There was a drug, she knew, that people used. She had read stories about women who were given this drug and then hurt . . . What was its name, the drug? She could not remember.

Standing up again, she moved carefully towards the door. She tried to put the light on, but it didn't work. The door was locked.

'Richard!' she shouted. There was no answer. Again she shouted, but her voice only sounded in the empty room.

Now she knew she was right to be afraid. What was Richard trying to do? What did he want from her? He must be mad and dangerous. She must escape, run away from here, from him. Now.

She went quickly to the window. It was locked too, of course. But looking down she saw that the room was above the front door of the house. She could see the small roof over the door just below her. She could get down onto the roof and jump to the ground from there. She must break the window – but how? She went back to the fire. Ah, a half burnt piece of wood. She could use that.

The glass in the window broke with a lot of noise. Richard would hear, for sure. Quickly, she climbed out and dropped down onto the small roof. 'That wasn't too bad,' she thought. 'Now for the big jump.' She looked down at the ground. It seemed a long way away.

Was that a sound in the room behind her? There was no time to lose. She shut her eyes and stepped over the side of the roof.

She landed hard on the ground. But she hadn't hurt herself. She stood up. Everything was OK. There was a shout in the room above the door. She must go. Fast.

The moon made it easy to see the road. As she ran, a sound came from Richard's house which made her blood run cold. It was a terrible, angry scream. She looked behind her at the house but there was nothing following her. Yet.

In front of her, the road was clear, the snow on the road shining in the grey light.

Then, a moment later, she saw a man coming towards her further down the road. He was holding a gun.

Without thinking, she turned from the road and ran across a field towards a high hill. She started to climb the hill. It was difficult in the dark and the snow. She held onto plants and small trees to stop herself falling. Soon her hands were cut. She used her clothes to clean the blood from her hands.

When she got to the top she realised that she was on Brynmawr Hill. Of course! Richard had said that his house was quite near Cynghordy House. Perhaps she could get back there. But it was locked, she remembered. The key was in her bag and she had left her bag in Richard's house. Oh God, what was she going to do? And what about Charlie? He must be very worried about her. What would he think?

Perhaps she should go to Tom's house. He lived near too, didn't he? But which way was it to his house? Looking around her on the hill, she had no idea where to go.

She was very tired. She must stop for a bit first. She must sit down and rest. She needed to think what to do. She had a terrible headache and her arms and legs were hurting. She could go no further. The ground was cold and wet with snow but she didn't care.

Just then she realised that an icy wind was blowing across the top of the hill. She was in the same place where she had taken the photographs on that first day, on the little hill. As she looked back at the way she had just come, the wind became stronger. The noise of the wind was in her ears and she could hear nothing else.

Then she saw that coming up the small hill towards her was a very large black animal. The moonlight lit up its eyes and they were burning like fires. When the animal saw her, it began to make a strange and terrible noise, like a wolf.

This was not a dream. This was real. She must run. But she could not move.

The animal was coming closer quickly, its great legs working to carry it. It was moving faster than the wind. Susie watched, unable to do anything. It was very near now and about to jump at her.

Suddenly, there was the sound of a gunshot.

The animal rose up on its back legs. It seemed more than three metres tall. Its lips were pulled back in a terrible smile and its large, dangerous teeth were white in the moonlight. Something silver could be seen in the hair of its stomach.

As Susie screamed, another shot rang out. A black hole seemed to open in the animal's body. It turned with a wild shout and ran towards the wood on its two back legs. At that moment, Susie realised something with a terrible certainty. What she had seen was not an animal. It was a man.

'Well, I'll be . . . !' a voice said behind her, a voice she knew was Tom's. 'Come on, young lady. We'd better take you home.'

Chapter 14   *Silver bullet*

It was a long time before Susie could stop shaking. She felt so cold. The worried faces of Tom and his wife Kathryn watched her as she drank the hot sweet tea. They were good people but she felt small and lost. They'd taken away her wet and bloody clothes. They'd put a blanket around her, like a child. She was in the warm light sitting-room of their house. She was safe now, after the darkness and danger.

Kathryn smiled at her. 'You'd better stay here with us, my dear.' She was quite worried about the young woman who was sitting and shaking on the sofa. Something terrible had happened. It was clear that Susie could not return to her holiday house.

'Tell me,' Kathryn wanted to know, 'Tom says he found you out walking about up on the hill. It's the middle of the night. Did something happen? What were you doing there?'

'I . . . I don't really know.' She was too tired to try to remember. She started to cry and cry. She couldn't stop.

'Now, Kathryn,' Tom said. 'See what you've done? No more questions now. Come on, my dear, you need to get to bed.'

That first night in Tom and Kathryn's house, Susie slept deeply and dreamlessly. Several times during the following morning Kathryn looked at her. She saw how white Susie's face was as she slept. Kathryn knew that she needed to sleep. She moved away quietly. Susie did not wake until the afternoon.

Slowly, in the days that followed, Susie began to return to the world again. But she couldn't remember much about what had happened.

She said to Kathryn, 'Someone . . . Richard . . . was taking me to see Charlie. We went to his house. Then I don't know what happened. Perhaps I went for a walk and got lost. I don't know. What must Charlie be thinking? Can I phone him?'

'Now there's no need to be worried about that husband of yours. Tom has already seen him and told him what happened.' Kathryn said to her.

'What did Tom tell Charlie?' Susie asked.

'Oh, that he found you up on Brynmawr Hill in the middle of the night while he was out hunting for the thing that's been killing his sheep,' Kathryn replied.

'What did Charlie say?'

'I don't know, my dear.' Kathryn looked at her. 'But I know Tom told him that you're fine. He promised your Charlie that you'll go and see him very soon, just as soon as you're strong again.'

'Charlie must think I've really gone mad,' Susie thought to herself. 'Perhaps I have.'

'I've lost my bag,' she said to Kathryn. 'I don't know where it is. My money's in it. And the key to Cynghordy House.' She felt stupid.

'Perhaps it's in your holiday house?' Kathryn said.

'I don't think so. I don't know,' Susie said, unhappily.

'Well, then, perhaps Richard's got it?' Kathryn said.

'Ah . . . yes . . . perhaps he has it,' Susie said finally. She realised that the sound of Richard's name made her feel strangely afraid. She started to shake a little.

'Now, now.' Kathryn put her arm around her. 'It's all right. Don't worry about it now. I'll ask Tom to go over to Richard's house and get your bag for you.'

Susie knew that she had been into a place of darkness. The Underworld. For a moment, she had wanted to stay there. Yet somehow she had escaped with her life. She didn't want to try to understand yet. It was too soon. She just knew that the place she had seen was dangerous. It was somewhere that living people do not usually go. If they do, they do not usually return.

*   *   *

A day or two later, Tom was sitting at the kitchen table, eating his dinner. Susie saw that her bag was on the table next to him. 'You got it, then?' she said.

'Yes,' he said, his mouth full of food. He kept his eyes on his plate. He didn't look at Susie. He knew what she was going to ask. He wasn't sure that he wanted to answer.

'Did Richard have it?' she asked.

'Er . . . well, yes . . .' Tom stopped, looking uncomfortable.

Something in Tom's voice made Susie ask another question. 'Did you see him, then?'

'No, he wasn't there.' Tom looked at the table. 'Strange thing is, no-one's seen Richard lately, you know. He hasn't been into the pub since that night,' replied Tom.

'Oh?'

'And what's even stranger . . .' Tom spoke very quietly. 'He told everyone, you know, in the pub, that he was working on his house.'

'Yes,' Susie said. 'He was. I saw it. A lot of it had fallen down and the windows were broken. He said he had to start building some of it again. There were a couple of rooms that were OK, I think.' She remembered a room full of large pictures.

'Well, this morning,' Tom began, 'I had to move my sheep down onto a field on the other side of the hill, down near Richard's house. So I decided to go and ask if he had your bag . . . '

'Go on,' Susie said.

'Well.' He looked carefully at her. 'If it ever was a house, it's not a house any more. It's fallen down. There's trees and grass growing on the stones, too. I went for a closer look. I'd say no-one's touched that place for years. No-one's been near it or done anything to it. It's just a mountain of stones. I'd say it's been like that for a hundred years or so.'

Tom's voice shook. Susie could hear that he was afraid of what he was saying. The hair on her skin stood up and a cold feeling went down her body.

'Where was the bag, Tom?' she asked finally.

'It was lying there, on the stones . . . and I found something else too,' he said softly. 'In the woods on the hill.'

'What?' Susie asked.

After a few seconds, Tom got up and went out of the room, returning with something in his hands. He put it on the table in front of Susie. Looking down, Susie saw that it was a large heavy black belt with a silver dog's face on it. Tom watched her closely. Her face had lost all its colour.

'Tom, I have to ask you something . . . ' she said slowly.

55

'What really happened up there on the hill? You know, that night when you found me? Was it a dog out after the sheep? And you shot it?'

'Perhaps,' Tom said. 'I was fairly sure I hit him. Not the first time, the second time I think . . . '

Susie looked at him. He hadn't answered the real question. 'Yes, I'm pretty sure I got him in the heart,' Tom went on. 'Strange thing was, I went to look the next day and . . . well, there was no blood or body, nothing . . . '

Then he said, 'You had a lucky escape. Lucky I had this. And some of these.' He held up his gun and a silver bullet. 'You know, he nearly got you,' Tom said.

'He?' Susie asked.

They looked at each other. They both knew that what they were thinking was impossible.

After a few moments, Susie said quietly, 'I'd like to see Charlie.'

'Sure, no problem,' Tom said. 'Kathryn's going shopping this afternoon, she said. She can take you in later.'

'Thanks, you've both been very kind, you know,' Susie said.

She thought about seeing Charlie and what she could say to him. She wanted to say that the days they'd spent together here had been good. In London they hadn't seen each other much in the last few months. They had such busy lives. She wanted to tell him she was sorry that he was hurt. Perhaps they could try again to have a holiday? And she wanted to talk about having a child some time. Not now, but soon.

Chapter 15 *Voice of the Beast*

From where I am now, the rivers are silver snakes. The fields are green squares and the trees are like small flowers. Below me, your world is just a map. I see the sheep – they are the size of stones on a beach. They are dirty and grey against the snow that still lies in the fields. The woods on the side of the hill are black as the night. A thin line of smoke rises from a house at the bottom of the hill. My hill.

Two women come out of the house. They look like toy people. They get into their toy car and I hear it start. It sounds like an angry fly. Shall I call to them? Just for fun? Just to see, even from here, if she is still afraid? I can see very well, you know. I have the eyes of a bird that kills.

So what happened to me, you may ask?

Do you remember what I said? No, probably not. I'll tell you again.

'There is nothing you can do to escape from us. You may think you can kill us with your silver bullets. But you cannot.'

Well, yes, OK, the farmer did hit me with his silver bullet. Then my body became a stone – one of the stones that the farmer passed, in fact, as he searched for me. If you think this sounds impossible, look carefully at the large stones that sit on hills in wild places. Look for the eyes and faces of the stones. Ask yourself what lies locked inside them.

I returned for a short time to the world of darkness and the undead. But as I have told you, I will always need the blood of living things. I will always need to move into your world. I cannot stay away. Bad luck for you.

'We just move from one body to another, from one place to another.'

This time, I'm tired. You cannot possibly understand how tired it makes me, time after time, having to find a new hiding place. So, no, I will not go again around the earth. I will stay here among these woods and fields.

Now I am one of the red kites that fly over the Welsh hills. One of those birds that look for animals to kill and eat. This is good. From where I am I can see everything.

It is true that my plan did not work as I wanted. She was stronger than I thought. She escaped from me when I thought she was mine. I made a mistake. My plan was not careful enough.

But there is something she does not yet know. And I will wait now for that something to happen.

Wait? What does that mean? That time passes? You people, I feel sorry for you. You talk of beginnings and endings. But the beginning and the end of the world are beyond your understanding. You are too stupid. Don't you know that the beginning is still happening? Those sounds that come from beyond the stars, that your scientists pick up on their radios – they think those sounds will show them how the world began. Actually, they are the last sounds of a timeless, lazy laugh. Your world is a great and terrible joke. And those strange animals that people talk of – the Loch Ness Monster in Scotland, the Yeti in the Himalayas, the Mono Grande in Brazil, the Chupacabras in Mexico, the Volkodlak in Central Europe – what are they? They are children of the darkness. They are part of the joke. They carry messages from the joker.

Sorry, I am forgetting. What was I going to say? You are waiting to know, aren't you? All right then, because you ask, I'll tell you.

She will have a child soon. When she looks through her camera at her baby, she will see that I am the father. For the camera does not lie, but shows the world as it really is. With her camera, she sees things that her eyes cannot see.

And I promise by my own father, Lykaon, who killed a child and gave it to the god, Zeus, to eat, that I will return to take what is mine.

Glossary of animals

page 8

wolf (pl. wolves)

page 11

goat

sheep

page 15

fox

red kite

Cambridge English Readers

Other titles available at Level 3:

Double Cross
by Philip Prowse

An attempted killing in Stockholm sends secret agent Monika Lundgren racing across the world. As she chases the would-be killer, she meets a mysterious football team, a rock musician, and a madman with dreams of world power . . .

The Ironing Man
by Colin Campbell

After moving to a small village in the country with her husband Tom, Marina finds herself isolated and bored while Tom's at work. She wishes she had someone to do the housework for her and, to her surprise, her wish comes true.

The House by the Sea
by Patricia Aspinall

A married couple, Carl and Linda Anderson, buy a weekend house by the sea. But one weekend, Linda does not arrive at the house and Carl begins to worry. What has happened to her? Who is the taxi driver that follows Carl? And how much do the people in the village really know?

Just Good Friends
by Penny Hancock

Stephany and Max go on holiday together for the first time

to get to know each other better. They go to Italy and stay with Carlo who is an old friend of Stephany's. But Carlo's wife is not very happy to see Stephany and the two couples soon find out why . . .

Two Lives
by Helen Naylor
In the small Welsh village of Tredonald, Megan and Huw fall in love. But is their love strong enough to last? Death, their families and the passing years are all against them.